No Tree For Christmas

THE STORY OF JESUS' BIRTH

By Marilyn Lashbrook

Illustrated by Stephanie McFetridge Britt

CANDLE
BOOKS

NO TREE FOR CHRISTMAS
will offer your child the
opportunity to feel the excitement
of the shepherds as they searched
for and found God's Son. The story
of Jesus' birth is told from a
different perspective emphasizing
the fact that Jesus is God and that
He is what Christmas is really
all about.

Your little one will enjoy
answering the questions
throughout the book after the story
has been told a time or two. Be
sure to pause after questions to
allow your child to fill in the
answers.

At the end of the story, why not
take a moment to worship with
your child with a one-sentence
prayer or by singing "Away in a
Manger."

First published in the UK by Candle Books Ltd. 1992.
Reprinted 1993, 1995, 1996, 1997
Distributed by SP Trust, Triangle Business Park,
Wendover Road, Stoke Mandeville, Aylesbury, Bucks, UK.

Coedition arranged by Angus Hudson Ltd., London.

Printed in Hong Kong.

ISBN 0 948902 57 4

All enquiries to Angus Hudson Ltd., Concorde House,
Grenville Place, Mill Hill, London NW7 3SA, England.
Telephone : +44 181 959 3668
Fax   : +44 181 959 3678

NO TREE FOR CHRISTMAS

THE STORY OF JESUS' BIRTH

By Marilyn Lashbrook

Illustrated by Stephanie McFetridge Britt

Taken from Luke 2

"Shh ... Did you hear that?"
The shepherds jumped up
and listened carefully.
What had they heard?

Was it a naughty lamb sneaking away?
No.

Was it a thief stealing wool for a coat?

No.

Was it a wild animal looking for supper?

No.

What could it be?

It was an angel!

The shepherds were so frightened
their knees were quaking

and their hands were shaking.
And they weren't faking!
They had never seen an angel before.

"Do not be afraid," said the angel.
"I have good news for you.
... happy news for all the world!"

"A Savior was born today.
He is the Lord!
"You will find Him in Bethlehem
sleeping in a manger."

When the angel went back to Heaven,
The shepherds went to look
for God's special baby.

This was the most exciting thing
they had ever done!

When they came to Bethlehem,
they searched the stables one by one.
Was this the place they were looking for?
No.

Was this the place they were looking for?
No.

Was THIS the place they were looking for?
No.

But they kept searching.
Do you think they found the right stable?

Yes!

This was it!

Here was the baby in a manger
just like the angel said.

The shepherds came closer
to look at this very special baby.

They were filled with wonder.
Why?

Because Baby Jesus was the Son of God.

He came to bring love and forgiveness
to people everywhere.

This was the very first Christmas,
and it was the best of all.

The shepherds did not need lighted trees
or brightly-wrapped presents
or candy-filled stockings to be happy.

JJ-clown $x1$ $x2$ Snell
Nico-Circus $x1$ $x2$ spanna

Backups
JJ=Top
Nico

JJ is a idiot
Nico is the best at being a idiot (Shake him).

They were happy just to see God's Son,
so they got down on their knees
to worship Him.

They thanked Him, and praised Him,
and said to Him, "We love You, Lord Jesus!"

ME TOO!
B O O K S

ME TOO!
R E A D E R S
